T0195840

GIVE ME SOME SUGAR

Spreading Kindness Everywhere

LORI ANN LEGGETTE

WestBow Press books may be ordered through booksellers or by contacting:

WestBow Press
A Division of Thomas Nelson & Zondervan
1663 Liberty Drive
Bloomington, IN 47403
www.westbowpress.com
844-714-3454

Scripture quotations taken from The Holy Bible, New International Version® NIV® Copyright © 1973 1978 1984 2011 by Biblica, Inc. TM. Used by permission. All rights reserved worldwide.

ISBN: 978-1-6642-7505-8 (sc)
ISBN: 978-1-6642-7506-5 (e)

Library of Congress Control Number: 2022914630

Print information available on the last page.

WestBow Press rev. date: 02/16/2023

WESTBOW
PRESS®
A DIVISION OF THOMAS NELSON
& ZONDERVAN

This book is dedicated to:
Johnetta Leggette
March 26, 1959 - November 28, 2018

Thank you for showing us
loving kindness.

Jeremiah 31:3 NIV

The LORD appeared to us in the past, saying: "I have loved you with an everlasting love; I have drawn you with unfailing kindness.

kind·ness
/ˈkīn(d)nəs/

noun

1. the quality of being friendly, generous, and considerate.

"he thanked them for their kindness and support"

I can't really decide on the pet I want to love and to be loved by. I could a get a rabbit, but I don't have time to clean a cage. A rabbit would be nice and cuddly. I could have a parrot that talks and sing songs all day. But where would it fly, what if it flies away?

Do I want a cat? They're nice, clean and quiet. I won't be able to walk a cat on a leash. I think I'd like to get a puppy. A puppy that stays small, fun and likes to run and play. I need a puppy that will keep me company night and day!

I hope my new puppy will be nice and kind. Just to give love and joy and won't really mind. I've got to find a puppy. While searching in pet stores, I've seen so many cute puppies. I'm praying God could just send me a sign.

I'll know him or her from the start because I'll feel the love in my heart.

My new puppy is happy to be in her new place called home. She's beautiful, courageous, and playful! But most of all, she's MINE!

I've got a list of names, but I haven't decided on the perfect name to call her.

Lily - ✘	Betsy - ✘	Raven - ✘
Hope - ✘	Priscilla - ✘	Jane - ✘
Dakota - ✘	Arizona - ✘	SUGAR – ✓

I'll call her "SUGAR!" She's
as sweet as can be.

SUGAR is like a "ray of sunshine" to so many people. Everywhere we go she's spreading kindness, love and happiness. She spreads her plain ole' SUGAR!

SUGAR loves to go to the grocery store and as soon as we get through the door. Here comes the people to gather all around to hold and love her and say, what a cutie I've found?

We met a lonely old lady who has no family in the store one day and she asked, "will you bring her to visit me every now and then? I have no family and I'd love to visit and play with her. I promised to bring SUGAR to play and stay one day.

I'm learning so much from SUGAR being in my life. She's shown me that GOD intended for us to spread love and kindness throughout our precious lives.

SUGAR loves to run and play with Jerrion, Caleb and the neighborhood children. SUGAR loves it when the boys throw her toy, she runs to get it, and brings the toy back.

"Give me some SUGAR," means it's okay for us to be kind to one another. SUGAR'S a puppy and she's walking in her GOD given PURPOSE. Why can't we?

Spreading kindness everywhere we go!

GOD used the following individuals and animals:

ELIJAH AND THE RAVENS
ELISHA AND THE BEARS
DANIEL AND THE LIONS
JESUS AND THE PALM
SUNDAY DONKEY
LORI AND SUGAR (CUTE,
SWEET AND KIND PUPPY)

Printed in the United States
by Baker & Taylor Publisher Services